smileitude™
Brightens Your Day
I0697478
"What is just a smile to me,
Sets another one free."
©2023
– Smileitude™

How to Make
Mom Smile

...with

smileitude™

Conversation Guide

This is a simple conversation guide meant for helping people come together.
It in no way replaces professional services or advice.
Every effort has been made in good faith to avoid any copyright infringements.
The publishers will be pleased to make good any omissions or rectify any
mistakes brought to their attention at the earliest opportunity.

How to Make Mom Smile...with smileitude™
Written by Livylyn Grace
On behalf of the Smileitude™ Team

Published by Livylyn Grace

IG @Livylyn.Grace

First paperback edition September 2023

For permissions contact: livylyn.grace@smileitude.com

In This Conversation Guide

Smileitude™ Introduction

What is Smileitude™?

Anyone can smile. But smileitude™ is beyond that. It is an attitude of more than just what one can see on the surface. It is about getting out of our own personal world and being deeply connected with others, working, not just toward our own interests and happiness - but for the happiness of others around us as well and making more time to do so together. It is a rewarding goal and fulfilling attitude of togetherness and unity as you are truly looking out for the interests of others. In other words, smileitude™ truly brightens your day and anyone else you choose to share it with because giving happiness brings happiness. But watch out! The smileitude™ attitude can be very contagious to those around us. So don't be surprised when you find others reciprocating the same unselfish smileitude™ right back at you! That is surely the type of "pandemic" (or might we call it smiledemic™) we would all surely welcome.

How to Use This Book:

Smileitude™ Conversation Prompts.
The Smileitude™ conversation prompts are simple conversation topics designed to help you get to know more about the ones you love. Some are for fun while others are meant to help you dig a little deeper to help you get to know your loved ones better. If you or your friend or loved one prefer journaling over conversation prompts, you might consider getting them the companion Smileitude™ Shared Activity-Journal.

Positive Awareness Through Smileitude™ Activities.
The Smileitude™ series can help you to personally get more connected with others around you. It can be an enjoyable, yet simple project to undertake with those you love and who you would like to make the strongest connections with. People who want this type of connection with others are the ones who we had in mind when designing this series. To this end, we have provided some simple Smileitude™ activities (some individual and some for teamwork) that tend to raise people's awareness of how their own positive efforts to act in a loving and unified way with and toward each other works for their own greater happiness and that of those around them whom they choose to share some smileitude™ with. Some simple charts are provided in the companion Smileitude™ Shared Activity-Journal (separate purchase from this book) so you can keep track of the activities you complete, and there is even room to create some of your own questions and activities.

About the Smileitude™ Series

Are you having trouble connecting with someone you love? Everyone sees the world from a different perspective. What makes another person feel secure? What makes them happy? What makes them feel special? What completes them? How can they learn the same about you? And, how can you learn ways to add to each others' happiness? The most important unit of society is the family. Close, upbuilding friends are also very important, sort of like the "family" we get to choose ourselves. What can help friends and families get more connected with each other in a positive way? A combination of clean, fun and searching questions and activities can help you get to know your loved ones better and learn how you can fit into each other's lives in a more complementary, meaningful way with a deep, satisfying friendship as the desired result. Good, face-to-face communication and activities along with sacrifice are key to making this happen. This is something that is needed now, in the day and age of social media, more than ever. This is especially so as we see a huge rise in adverse effects on the mental health and wellbeing of more and more people, particularly our youths. And the multiple Smileitude™ series of Conversation Guides and Handbooks (as well as the guided activity-journals which you can gift to your friends or loved ones) are all designed to assist you in this exciting endeavor to find new ways to help you accomplish this noble purpose while learning to keep social media in its place. Some of you may also enjoy getting a Smileitude™ Activity-Journal for each of you to fill out and then swapping them once they are completed so you can both read about what really makes your friend or loved one happy and then setting goals to act on that information to help grow your friendships - unselfishly as a team. The journaling prompts can also be used as a means of extending conversation once the questions are completed.

Is it your brother you would like to get to know better? Gift them the Smileitude™ "Brother" Activity-Journal edition. Your sister? Get one for them too in the "Sister" edition! (And if you are either the brother or the sister, you could get that edition for you to write in your own answers to share with your sibling(s) as well.) Parents may also like to get the sibling editions for each of their children so that: 1) they can share themselves with each other, and 2) to help them learn communication skills that can last a lifetime. There are parent, child, sibling, friend and other family editions. The Smileitude™ "Couples" edition can be used for anyone you are serious about to help in strengthening your relationship further, as many wish to do before they get more serious about marriage and starting a family together. Married couples might also enjoy it. You may wish to explore any of our other books in this series, What Makes You Smile? ...with Smileitude™, as well so that you can find more ways to grow closer to other dear friends and loved ones and really connect with one another. (See back pages for more books in this expanding series of journals, guides and handbooks.)

We look forward to helping you enjoy this journey together with each person you hold dear.

And remember - Smileitude™ brightens your day as well as everyone else whom you share it with!

Yours Truly,
The Smileitude™ Team

Section 1:
MOM

Conversation Prompts to Ask

Mom

About Mom

smileitude™
Brightens Your Day

"A smileitude™ day,
Keeps the clouds at bay."

©2023

— Smileitude™

What is your favorite thing about being a mother? What has been the most challenging thing to you about being a mom? How have you overcome it?

Did you always want to have children? What makes you the most happy that you did?

What do you miss most about being a child? ...a teenager? What do you NOT miss about being a child? ...a teenager?

In what ways has life in this world changed since you were a child? ...a teenager?

What is your favorite childhood memory?

What do you wish you would have done differently in your life? How do you imagine your life would be different now if you had?

Who was your all-time favorite teacher? What did you appreciate most about them? How did they help shape you into the person you are today?

Which person from your childhood do you feel shaped your life the most? How so?

Which book author gave you the most childhood enjoyment? Why? How do they affect your life to this day?

Is there a favorite childhood TV show that you grew up on? How do you think it affects your view of life to this day? Which character did you relate to the most?

What awards have you won? Can you tell me what all you did to accomplish this?

If a movie or TV show were made about you, who would play you? What would be its theme? What would make it exciting?

What three things are you most grateful for? Why are you grateful for these things? How do you feel they make your life better?

If you could trade places with anyone throughout history, who would it be? Why them?

What kind of atmosphere makes you feel most secure? Can you describe in detail the perfect environment?

Who was your childhood best friend? What did you do together for fun? How do they affect your life to this day? Do you still keep in touch?

If you could travel back in time to your childhood self, what advice would you give yourself to do differently that you feel could make you an even better person than you already are?

What helps to keep you feeling most balanced when things get tough? How can I help you when things get to this point?

What is the biggest lesson you have learned from past mistakes that has made you a better person today?

What is the smartest decision you have ever made? How do you imagine your life would be now if you had decided differently?

Which pet was your favorite growing up?
What did you like most about it?
How did having a pet help you as a person?

If one day you woke up as the absolute master of any profession or hobby, what would you like it to be?
What would you hope to accomplish with that new skill?

What do you obsess over most nowadays?
What about when you were young?

How did your friends growing up help shape you into the person you are today?

smileitude

Do you enjoy writing? What was your favorite story/
poem/etc. you ever wrote? Or, is there something you
would like to write about?

What is the best thing that a friend has ever done for
you? Why do you appreciate what they did? Were you
ever able to do something kind in return, or would you
like to have? What would/did you do for them?

What is the best thing you have ever done for a friend?
How did that turn out? How did it contribute to helping
you feel good about yourself for helping them?

What is the most important lesson in general that you
feel living through your life could teach others?

If you could go back in time and ask anyone a question,
who would it be? What question would you ask?
How do you think they might respond?
How would this help you today?

If you could solve any problem in today's world, what
would it be? Why that problem?
How would you go about it?

What is your secret "sauce" to helping others feel good
about themselves?

What is the nicest thing you have ever done for a
stranger? How did they respond?
How did that make you feel?

Which possession is most dear to you?
Why do you value it?

Which aroma takes you back to your happiest moments
as a child?
What do you remember most about those times?

When you're feeling anxious, what is the first thing you
do to try to remedy the situation?

What would you like to be remembered most for?

What is the best thing that ever happened to you as a
child?

What is the best thing that ever happened to you as a
teenager?

What is the best thing that ever happened to you as an
adult?

What is the best thing that ever happened to you all
around?

smileitude

smileitude™
Brightens Your Day
"Your smiling glow,
Makes my happiness flow."
©2023
– Smileitude™

Section 1b: Mom

Activity

#1 - Smileitude™ Awareness

Description

For one month, keep track of how much time you spend each week "connected" on devices (e.g. - computer or video games, surfing the web, social media, TV, etc) versus how much time you spend on face-to-face, in-person activities (without using electronic devices) together with the ones you love (e.g. - - playing board games together, taking walks together, having actual in-person conversations, doing hobbies/reading aloud together, etc). At the end of one month evaluate to see where improvement could be made in spending truly connected time together with your friend/loved one (with no electronic devices) and explore different ways/times you can make it happen with them. Consider making a commitment to yourself to do this and putting it in writing.. (You may also wish to turn this into a team activity with different ones you love where you both/all make a commitment towards one another in this effort.)

Section 2: US

Conversation Prompts to Ask

Mom

About "Us"

What is your favorite part of our friendship and why?

Since raising children is about shaping them into productive members of society, what type of internal moral legacy do you hope to instill (or, hope you have instilled) in me?

What lesson from your life would you like to pass on to me most?

Do you feel I am understanding enough? What would you like for me to understand more about you?

Is there any area in which you wish I were more like you? How would this benefit me?

Is there any area that you wish you were more like me? Why do you feel that way?

How would you describe our relationship/friendship to others?

How do you think we could improve our friendship/relationship?

Is there anything that you would like for me to do more of with you?

What is the ultimate advice you would like to offer me about growing up? (Or, about the time of life I am in?)

What is the most important advice you would like to offer me about starting/nurturing my own family?

What other important advice would you like to share with me?

What makes you feel most connected to me?
What do you need most from me?

What do I do that makes you happy?
How does that make you happy?
What can I do to help you be happier?

What will you remember most about me after I grow up and have my own family? (Or, What do you remember most about me when I was living at home?)

What quality about me do you admire most?
Why? What quality could I improve on?

If it were possible for us to switch places for a day, what do you think would happen? What might go right? What might go wrong?

What do you feel is our best trait in common?
How do you think this helps us?

Imagine you and I could go anywhere and have the best day ever. Where would our journey lead us? What would we do?

At what age did I challenge you the most as your child? Is there anything you wish you would have done differently?

What is the most important advice you would like to offer me about social media vs real friends?

How do you think our differences benefit us both?

What advice do you have for helping me choose good friends?

What is your fondest memory of me when I was young/younger?

Do you feel there is anything I obsess over too much?
Any advice to help me with this?

What do you feel I excel at that makes you proud?

What is the next thing you would like to see me excel at?

Do you think I make a good parent (or, will make a good parent someday)? Why?

What is the best thing that ever happened to us and our relationship while I was growing up?

What is the best thing that ever happened to us and our relationship since I became an adult?

In what way(s) would you like to spend more time together now?

What would you like to know more of about me?

Do you feel I give you enough time/space to pursue your own interests?

What do you need most from me as your child right now?

What challenges are you facing right now? And how can I support you through them?

Is there any particular experience we have shared that you feel drew us closer together ? When was this? What made it so special to you?

What is the most courageous thing you have ever had to do for me as my parent?

What is one thing that you wanted us to pursue together but we never got the chance to?

What was most typical aspect of raising me? (Typical of what a parent might expect.)

What was the least typical aspect of raising me?

Section 2b:
Us
Activities

Smileitude™ Activity

#2 - Togetherness Practice

Description

For this activity, designate a week or weekend (or even just a day if that is all the time you have to work with practically) each month where you implement together with your loved one ways you each brainstormed (in the previous activity) to help you put away all your electronic devices and spend that time being truly connected with each other. You might find it fulfilling to pursue a "face-to-face" hobby together during this time. Perhaps some months this special time of true togetherness can be done by means of a vacation get away or outdoor excursions. Whereas other times you might just feel like staying in together and finding things (e.g. - board games, conversations, hobbies...even projects that needs done around the house) to fill your time together. Either way, if each one works toward making it a success, such times can become most fulfilling and memorable times of togetherness. Learning to do things together as a team in a unified effort makes for great character building!

#3 - Focus on Us

Spend some time as a regular project writing down happy times you have had together as a family or as friends in the past and as you have them moving forward. Include what made those times enjoyable to you both/all. You can do this in a Smileitude™ Family Journal or write them down on slips of paper and keep them in a decorative can, jar or box. You may even wish to include some photos of the events. Then, when you are feeling tense, either as individuals or together (perhaps even as parent/child, if/when caregiving), you will have a rich smileitude™ "bank" to pull a few of the slips/photos out to reflect on together, almost like enjoying a "joint savings" account of happiness together. Consider how recent circumstances have contributed to the current stresses and how you can both (all) do some give and take in order to make the needed sacrifices that will help pull you together back into that same, or even better, peaceful state of being. Why wait! You can also work together proactively by picking a time every month to spend reminiscing over a few of those happy moments to keep your love for each other strong so that you are prepared for when such troubles arise.

#4 - Use What You Have Learned About Each Other

When you are both (all) in a positive frame of mind, take turns choosing a question from one of the sections in this book that you would like to explore more in depth by talking together about that particular topic. Be sure to approach the topic from a mutually positive and understanding point of view and not in such a way that causes one or the other of you to feel alienated in any way. Always remember that all smileitude™ activities are meant to encourage a positive atmosphere by looking for the good in each other, respecting the dignity of the other person and building each other up. Of course, it is always best to discuss any sensitive matters in private and with a mutual spirit of mildness. Consider doing this as a regular activity, one question at a time or by exploring other questions on new topics.

Section 3: FAMILY

Conversation Prompts to Ask

Mom

About Family

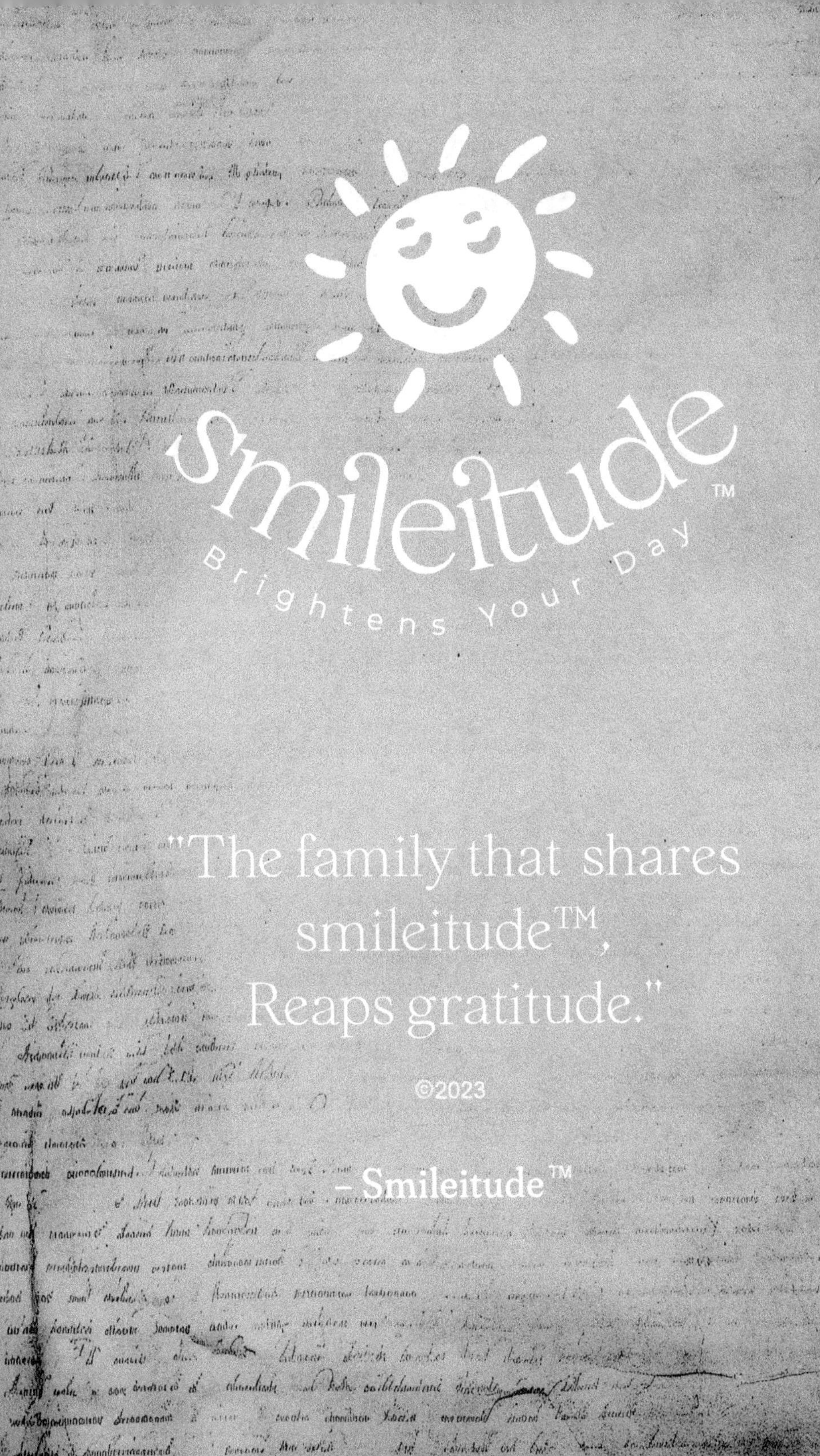
smileitude™
Brightens Your Day
"The family that shares
smileitude™,
Reaps gratitude."
©2023
– Smileitude™

How do you feel I contribute most to our family?
How do you feel you contribute most?

If a movie were made about our family, who do you think
would play each of us? What would be its theme? What
special ending do you wish you could make happen?

If our family inspired and became a reality show what
would it be called? What would be its theme?

Which of our family trips do you remember most? What
is your favorite memory from that trip?

Which of your family trips as a child do you remember
most? What is your favorite memory from that trip?

What is your favorite memory of your Mom and Dad?
Can you describe what happened?

What is your favorite memory of our whole family
together? What happened that made it special?

What is the nicest thing your parents have ever done for
you? How did this affect your life?

What do you appreciate most about your parents with regard to your upbringing? What effect has this had on you into your adulthood?

What do you wish your parents had understood more about you growing up? How do you think it would have made your life different if they had understood this?

What sort of habits does our family have that you love most? What sets us apart from other families?

Which habits do you think we could improve on as a family that would help everyone to be happier?

What makes you feel most connected to our family? Do you feel we have such moments often enough? If not, how could we make it happen more?

How would you describe our family relationship to your friends? Is there anything you would like for us to improve on together?

What is your favorite story about growing up with my aunt(s)/uncle(s) that you would like to share with me?

What about our family do you feel has helped you to be a better person? What do you need most from the family?

What lesson from your childhood do you think your children and grandchildren could benefit learning from the most? How would you help us/them comprehend it as we/they grow up?

What lesson from your teens do you think your children and grandchildren could benefit from the most to help them become happy, well-rounded adults? How would you go about teaching them this lesson?

What are the most important values in your life that you hope you pass down to your children? How have these values impacted your own life?

What question(s) would you like to go back in time and ask your great, great grandmother(s)/grandfather(s)? Why that/those question(s)?

If a movie was made about our heritage/ancestors what do you imagine would be its theme?
Which actors might play our ancestors?

What is your favorite recipe of your Mom's? Your Dad's?
Why do you like those recipe(s) so much?
Would you like to be able to pass the recipe(s) on to your own children?

Who do you think I will turn out to be more like, you or Dad?

If we could do any business together as a family what business would you choose? Why that business?

Since children are not born with a manual for parents to raise them what have you found to be your best source of guidance in raising yours?

What is your fondest memory of us children together when we were young/younger?

Who in our ancestry (e.g. - great, great grandparents or great/grand aunts/uncles, etc) that I never got the chance to meet do you wish I could have met most? What did you appreciate most about them?

What is one thing you wish you could have done for our family that you couldn't make happen?

What is the nicest thing you have ever done for your parents? Can you describe their reaction/how it went?

Were family traditions important for your family growing up? How have these shaped your life today? If you do not have these traditions today, would you like to? Why/ Why not?

Is there a family tradition that would be all our own that you feel we should start now? How do you think this tradition would help our family be closer?

What family traditions do you think you would have enjoyed?

What does our family share that differs from anything anyone else has? How do you feel this has helped our family grow over the years?

What is the most important thing we could ever do together as a family?

What do you think makes the family unit the most important unit of society?

What accomplishment do you think would bring our family even closer?

What do you think is the best thing that ever happened to us as a family?

What would you like for the family to be more involved with in your life in general?

What would you like for the family to be less involved with in your life in general?

What hobby would you like for our family to pursue together?

Section 3b:
Family

Activities

#5 - Giving Makes for Happiness Practice

It never hurts to spend some time together to boost your confidence as a family as to what you can accomplish as a team helping others. Pick a time each week or month to consider who of your friends, neighbors or loved ones might be in need and then act on that need. Whether it is simply telling something to them as a word of encouragement, spoken or by letter or greeting card, when going through a difficult time or solving some practical need that they do not have the means to solve by themselves, it can make for a truly enriching and character building experience together. One that can, not only help you grow as a family, but also bring you closer to another human being in the process, spreading some smileitude™ along the way. Such projects have contributed to the happiness of many from both sides, to the ones receiving such acts of kindness as well as the ones giving of themselves.

#6 - Everything We Know

Description

This is a fun activity to simply break the ice and get each other talking. Your friend or loved one might even have some unique, hidden gems inside that you could learn from. Set a timer for 2 minutes. One of you picks a fun/interesting topic (e.g. - an animal(s), flowers, other nature topics, geography, knock knock jokes, hobbies, skills, etc.) and asks the other to tell you everything they can that they know about your chosen topic in 2 minutes. Then, start the timer and let them start talking. Keep track of how many different details they give about the chosen topic. Afterwards, you can pick a new topic and switch who does the asking and answering. See who knew the most details about the topic they were given. This activity can be enjoyable with just a couple of people or with a group of friends and/or other family members. (Clue: The game is more fun if you ask each other about topics that are a bit challenging but that they also enjoy...and hopefully know at least something about in order to keep the game moving. Alternatively, each of you can prepare some topics ahead of time with each other in mind and write them on slips of paper, then put them in a hat or other container and mix them up well. Each person can grab one slip of paper out of the container when it is their turn to do the answering.)

Section 4: Effective Communication, Community

And BONUS Activities!

smileitude™
Brightens Your Day
"Spread smileitude™, Receive gratitude."
©2023
– Smileitude™

Learning Effective Communication

Plans. That is how every building being constructed is started. Without the proper blueprint, nothing can move forward progressively and successfully. The same is true when it comes to building strong family relationships, but this could even be said when it comes to building close friendships. We can't just assume that everyone is born with effective communication skills, particularly in a family with young children. This is a skill that is typically learned in the home.

The biggest aspect of forming close relationships with friends and family is making time to spend with each other in meaningful, face-to-face communication, which will, of course, vary depending on age. Do you have a plan for incorporating this into your regular family routine and activities so that you can draw closer as a family? What about with your friends? Do you include time for activities which encourage moments for open and relaxed communication with them as well? This is the kind of communication where we set aside our electronic devices, television included, and make each other feel important by giving the ones we love our full, face-to-face attention along with understanding and empathy so we can help each other through our darkest days and share some of our most joyful times as well.

Some families have chosen to make dinnertime every day their special time to enjoy talking with each other without distractions. They have topics for discussion or simply share the best/worst parts of their day with each other, giving everyone a chance to talk about their concerns and helping them to feel heard. For families, this can really help children to feel more secure because they sense that they are supported from a young and tender age. Friends might consider having similar regular times together as well.

Whatever time and activity each family chooses that is best for their family and/or friends in this endeavor, and as long as everyone is looking out for the best interests of the other person(s) and not just their own, and they have a plan set in place to make all this happen, it is possible to improve our relationships with our family and friends, making them successful and strong so they can withstand the tests of time. And when all involved strive for this end, it is possible to share a common feeling of deep smileitude™ satisfaction along the way.

Please enjoy the following communication tips, as well as activities, charts and templates, to help you continue in your development of togetherness with your family and friends.

<u>Communicating With The Ones We Love</u>
<u>Questions and Tips for Personal Reflection and Application</u>

These are questions that are mostly for personal reflection, but can also be used as "food for thought" when priming ourselves for how to approach a discussion on a sensitive issue. Often, it is just best to back up and think about things from a broader perspective, especially since we all have an inborn tendency to only think about things from our own personal view of things. Yet there is so much more that we need to take into consideration. This is often easier said than done. But with some regular reflection on the following questions and tips along with self-discipline and practice, it is not so hard to broaden our horizons. It can be done. It is something we all need to work on. Just be sure to give yourself (and your friend or loved one) some space for mess-ups...because they happen. No one is perfect. What is important is that you are both (all) actively working together toward improvement so that you can ultimately share with each other the wonderful spirit of smileitude™ more fully - and enjoy even more peace with your friend/loved one(s) along the way.

<u>The following questions center around things to consider when dealing with a sensitive issue (perhaps even one that could turn or has turned into an argument in the past)</u>:

1) Is this something I can simply let go? Is it worth stirring up anger in my friend or loved one or possibly hurting them?

2) What might I/we lose if I approach this in the wrong frame of mind? Our discussions will usually end in the same attitude we begin them with. So a good start is of prime importance for good, healthy communication.

3) Will I really be losing anything if I just forgive it and forget it?

4) Am I even going to remember this (whatever was said/done that offended me) a year from now? What about in two years? In ten years? Will it even make a difference in just a few weeks? If not, then it might be a good idea to refer to question 1 and just let it go.

5) Is this issue really worth tearing down my relationship/friendship with this person that we have worked so hard and long to build up?

6) What might I have done that has contributed to this problem/argument?

7) Can I be the one to take the lead in showing honor and respect to this person? Is arguing with them really being respectful? (Especially if it is something that has become a pattern?)

8) How can I turn this around into a positive "issue"? (i.e. - What is the goal I really want to achieve, and how can I go about it differently? How can it be turned into what is in the best interests of both/all of us?)

<u>And if the subject is something you simply cannot let go of after sincerely considering the questions above, you might ask yourself these questions:</u>

    9) Might there be a better time to discuss this topic for this person that I love so much? (And can I perhaps approach them when I am more relaxed as well and have thought out the best and most loving approach I can take to this problem?)

    10) Am I being too critical or expecting things to be done only "my way"? Am I expecting too much? Why?

    11) What is at the real root of what I am feeling? Sometimes, if we can figure this out, we can take some of the heat away from the issue and how we deal with it.
Use your imagination to see how you can make this happen.
As some examples, you could try one, or both, of the following suggestions:

    - Imagine someone whom you have a high regard for (best friend, favorite teacher, etc.) How might you approach them with a related issue?

    - Imagine you are speaking with your employer over a similar issue. How would you discuss the problem with them?
Sometimes, doing a mental exercise like this can separate our emotions from the problem and help us to think of a solution with a clearer head since we would most likely be more respectful in both of these scenarios than with our family, and sometimes even our friends, who are our closest "neighbors." We might even realize (in some cases) that our problem isn't as big as we thought it was and it might simply "melt away" when doing an exercise similar to the two above.

<u>Tips for approaching the individual whom we are upset with:</u>

    1) Try calmly, kindly and openly using the phrase "When you (say/do such-and-such) it makes me feel (such-and-such a way.)"

    2) If you have trouble getting yourself in a calm frame of mind when something is said or done that upsets you, take a deep breath and step away from the situation for a bit. Maybe go for a walk, read a book or play a quick game to get your mind off of the subject. Then, when you are calm, decide whether the topic needs further discussion or could just be let go. If you still feel you cannot let it go, follow the suggestions from questions 9-11 above.

    3) Another way to clear your head mentally when in a situation that has the potential to cause a heated argument is to try imagining for a moment that you are solving this problem from a different perspective than your own. The following are some possible mental scenarios you might consider using:

        a) If you had two children, or perhaps your child and their best friend, who were arguing with each other over the same (or similar) issue to what you are dealing with in the present, without taking sides, how would you help them to solve it?

b) A step further away might be to imagine how a respected and level-headed friend would deal with her child/children concerning the same issue.

c) Similar to options "a" and "b" above, switch it up and think about it from an employer/employee(s) perspective. How would you help two employees with a similar rift between them?

d) Try using your own imagination to come up with any other type of scenario that separates your emotions from the issue at hand so that you can deal with your own situation calmly and rationally.

Next, try applying the solution you imagine might have worked in that situation to the problem you are presently dealing with in connection with your loved one. By separating yourself mentally from the situation at hand using the situation you imagine, you might even begin to see that your problem isn't as big as you originally thought, which could serve to calm you down even more.

<u>Tips for helping prevent tension from developing in the first place</u>:

1) Try having a weekly time set aside where you can discuss your feelings and what you expect from each other in a calm and loving way. Use tips discussed in this section already to help in approaching each other calmly. For instance, speaking to each other in the same calm manner you might approach someone else whom you have high regard/respect for. Perhaps if you kindly and lovingly let each other know your personal needs during a calm and relaxed moment together, you won't feel the need to "force" each other to meet those needs while in the heat of an argument. Then work hard to try to apply some of those suggestions to help meet each other's needs. A great way to overcome sensitive issues and let each other know you are committed to making improvements is to voice what you feel you can personally work on to make things better and then follow through. Above all, be sure to consider yourselves as a team.

2) Try reminding yourself of the other person's good points regularly. The more positively you think about them as a person, the more respectful of an attitude you will approach them with.

3) Ask yourself "How is my tone when speaking to my friend/ loved one? Is it in such a way that automatically puts them in defensive mode? If so, might I (intentionally or unintentionally) simply be seeking or starting an argument?"

4) Concerning the point above, you might even want to ask your friend/loved one how your tone of voice sounds to them. This is something we may not even realize about ourselves. So it helps to see things from the other's perspective. It takes courage. But you might find that it is well worth the sacrifice.

5) After applying the suggestion above, try considering some ways of changing your tone of voice. Often, our tone of voice

reflects how we really feel about a person or a judgment we have made about them or something they say or do (or said or did.) You also may wish to try applying point 2 above, reminding yourself of their good points and why you love and/or appreciate them. Reflect on these good points often, especially when you start to feel upset with them. In addition, you might be surprised at how having some pictures on display of you and that person having a good time together can help get you in a better frame of mind as well. Or you might pull out an album you have with pictures of the two of you and take some time to reflect on your friendship/relationship and why it is worth working hard for.

6) Learn to be patient. After all, we appreciate when others are patient with us when we make mistakes. None of us are perfect. So the more understanding we have of this, the less likely we are to be too critical of each other. It also helps us to slow down and want to understand the other person's point of view.

7) Learn to forgive. A good, close friendship/relationship is impossible without a large measure of forgiveness. Are you a good forgiver? If not, can you work toward becoming one? Every functional relationship has two genuine and sincerely good forgivers on each side.

8) Be generous. Think, "How can I make this person happy/happier?" When we do so, and follow through with applying what we learn can make them happy (we might need to ask them every now and then, since people do change), often the other person will also be moved to be more generous toward us in return due to the example we set. Smileitude™ is impossible without this quality, as well as most of the points discussed above.

9) Consider other qualities you see in individuals whom you know have an exceptional tendency to be able to keep a level head when dealing with tense situations, and try to work at imitating these qualities in your daily life. Some qualities you might see in such individuals are characteristics like the following: genuine love for others; a joyful countenance that they like to share with others; a peaceful state of mind that they use to contribute to the peace of those around them; a generally kind and good-hearted disposition; and mildness and control over their own emotional state of mind. You might even ask them what helps them to display such beautiful qualities and keep their calm so effectively and what they do when something or someone threatens to dismantle their composure (which happens to everyone at some point in time.)

And if everything else fails to work, remember that a little well-placed, well-intentioned humor goes a long way in defusing a tense situation. Of course, it's very important to be thoughtful about this and be sure to not use humor that would cause any resentment in the other person.

Smileitude™ Activity

Bonus Smileitude™ Activity #1:
Community Practice
(Individually or Together)

Description

Is smileitude™ perhaps an attitude you can spread around you everywhere you go? Sometimes, all we need to do is break free from our own head/world/phone and try to briefly enter another person's world. It might even help us begin to see things in our own life in a whole new light. You might try the following activities/kindly gestures to help you reach out:

-- Simply offer others you see a genuine smile, meaning where you give someone a warm smile while making eye contact for at least a few seconds, as you encounter them when out shopping, perhaps even giving them a kind greeting. It's a good idea not to stare so long you make them uncomfortable, but just enough to show you care. Pay attention to what effect it has on them. You might just see your own power to brighten a stranger's day with smileitude™. And you never know when they might have actually really needed that boost. (Plus, just smiling to others in such a way is known to lift a person's own spirits as well.)
-- Incorporating the above gesture, go a step further and open the door for someone, or, if the doors are automatic, simply allow them to enter first.

Bonus Smileitude™ Activity #2:
The Smileitude™ Around You

Description

In this book so far we have focused on learning to project the smileitude™ attitude toward others. Now, last but not least, let's focus a little on the smileitude™ you <u>find around you</u>. Try locating people who genuinely like to help others. Once you locate them don't be afraid to ask what helps them display such a spirit of kindness toward others, even strangers. Then, see if you can apply some of what has helped them in your own life. Try not to limit your search to those whom you naturally expect such genuine kindness from. You might be surprised at those who you do not think would display it, yet, upon closer inspection, you find that they show a smileitude™-like attitude even more than some whom you expect it from. It may take some time to truly identify such people since smileitude™ is not simply something you see on the surface. You might have to "dig" a little (gently and patiently, of course.) But such people are out there. And I'm sure they are waiting to share their genuine spirit of smileitude™-like kindness with you. And, if you will allow them to, they will likely be happy to share their reasons for exhibiting such joy at all times of the year.

Keep track of what has helped such ones to maintain such a smileitude™-like attitude. Then share what you learn with your friends and family.

Conclusion

The multiple Smileitude™ series of books consist of conversation guides, handbooks and shared activity-journals which are meant to encourage an atmosphere of security, joy and connectedness among family and friends in as simple a manner as possible with a little bit of fun along the way.

We hope that this journey we have taken you on with Smileitude™ by means of this conversation guide and possibly its coordinating activity-journal for your friend or loved one has helped you to get started along this path and that you can continue to find ways to grow in your friendships and family togetherness moving forward. We also hope that you find benefit from this experience for years to come as well as benefit from our other books in this series for all your close friends and family whom you would like to get to know better or simply feel a bit more connected with. More of such meaningful relationships among family and friends can go a long way in a world filled with so much uncertainty and even loneliness for some. Sometimes it just helps to have a gentle nudge in the right direction.

With just a few questions and activities, and some basic reminders in understanding the foundation of good communication, many have been able to improve relationships with their closest neighbors, their family, and even with close friends. We encourage you to make it your goal to continue to find solutions that work for you and those whom you are close to.

You might also be interested in taking a look at some of our books that first inspired the Smileitude™ series on the next few pages to see which of your family and friends might appreciate them. These are the shared activity-journals which are complimented by the Smileitude™ series of Conversation Guides, like this one. We wish you many happy Smileitude™ journeys ahead together with your loved ones!

The Smileitude™ Team

Disclaimer: This book is NOT intended to replace professional advice. It is not intended as a psychology book. It is merely intended to help bring people together and help them share some happiness and positivity with those around them. When put to its intended use, much of the success of this book and its activities and question prompts will still depend on how much effort and sincerity each individual puts into applying the suggestions. Therefore, individual results will vary.

What Makes
You Smile...?
...with
smileitude™
Mom

What Makes
You Smile...?
...with
smileitude™
Sister

What Makes
You Smile...?
...with
smileitude™
Daughter

What Makes
You Smile...?
...with
smileitude™
Dad

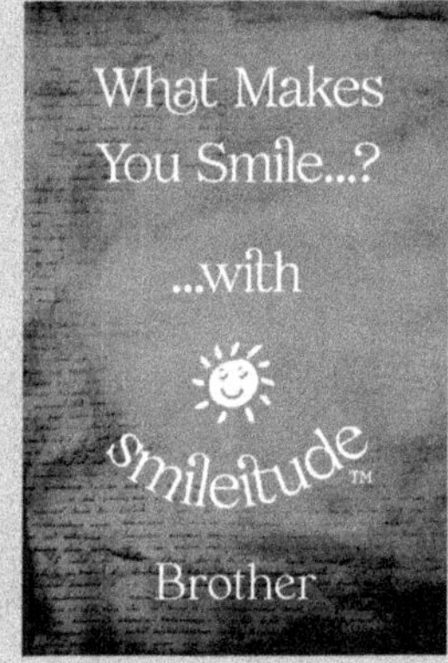
What Makes
You Smile...?
...with
smileitude™
Brother

What Makes
You Smile...?
...with
smileitude™
Son

What Makes
You Smile...?
...with
smileitude™
Couples

What Makes
You Smile...?
...with
smileitude™
Grandma

What Makes
You Smile...?
...with
smileitude™
Grandpa

The Smileitude™ Series

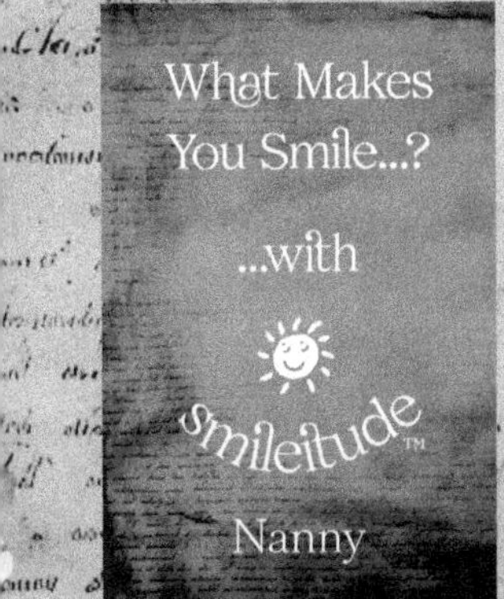

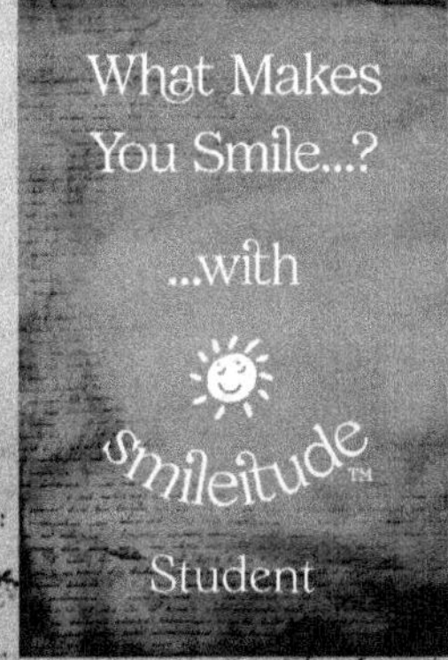

smileitude™
Brightens Your Day
"Sharing the key to another one's
happiness,
Is like turning the key to your own."
©2023
– Smileitude™